D1095184

Weaving on Cardboard

Also by Marthann Alexander

SIMPLE WEAVING

MARTHANN ALEXANDER

Weaving on Cardboard

Simple Looms to Make & Use

Taplinger Publishing Company / New York

Published in 1972 by
TAPLINGER PUBLISHING CO., INC.
New York, New York

Library of Congress Catalog Card Number: 70-164416

ISBN 0-8008-8120-6

Designed by Lynn Braswell

Contents

Illustrations

Introduction

Creative, inexpensive handwork is a must for children and adults. The use of yarns, string, and threads presents an opportunity for anyone to express himself in design and color. It is a thrill as one weaves to see the threads develop into an original fabric.

The weaving devices presented here are to give the inexperienced, as well as the experienced, ideas on ways to produce fabric without conventional looms.

The methods are not all weaving techniques in the strictest sense of the word, but they still produce cords, bands, and fabrics of very simple construction. Emphasis has been placed on the simplicity of the weaving device and the availability of the materials used. Very few special tools are needed to construct the so-called looms presented here. The cardboard recommended is the stiff carton type of board with the corrugations covered on both sides, presenting smooth outside surfaces. The recommended method of cutting it to the desired size is with the use of a serrated slicing knife.

These methods have been successfully used in teaching weaving to school children and to adults. Children in the middle grades take an immediate interest in weaving and succeed quickly.

The best results are obtained by reading through an entire chapter before the cardboard loom is constructed. Then carefully follow the directions given for preparing the cardboard base. I cannot emphasize too greatly the value of choosing from an array of threads, yarns, and colors. One good method is to ask a group to bring in all the odds and ends of yarns and threads they can find. Tiny bits of brilliant color can be combined successfully with other bits of color to produce weaving that is really exciting and original.

The material suggested here is based on notes gathered and used by the author over a period of years, both as a student of weaving in the United States and as a traveler studying weaving in Guatemala and Mexico. Some of the material was used in an original research paper for a Master's Degree in Art Education.

Most of the photographs are taken from the viewpoint of the weaver, thus showing the cardboard as it actually appears to the worker.

Weaving on Cardboard

1

Weaving a Place Mat on Cardboard

There is a method of weaving a flat mat on a piece of corrugated cardboard, which can easily be cut from a large carton. The cardboard should be smooth and unmarred. A suitable size for a place mat is 12-by-18 inches.

Measure the cardboard and cut with a serrated knife along a penciled line. Measure and mark ½ -inch intervals around all four edges, ½ inch from the cut edge. Punch the holes in the cardboard with a sharp darning needle or a thin nail. Tie a piece of cotton string at one corner and bind the edges with a single binding thread in each hole, sewing around the cardboard twice to make a continuous binder cord. A good material to use would be carpet warp, but since these binding strings are to be cut off to release the finished piece of fabric, any binding material may be used.

Begin to warp the cardboard loom by tying onto a corner a 3-yard piece of heavy yarn. Use a heavy yarn

1 / Warping a place mat loom

needle to bring the warp thread across the length of the cardboard and through the opposite string loop, then back through the first, or tying-on, loop. This puts a double thread from one end of the cardboard to the other. (See Illustration 1.) By threading back through the first loop before going on to the next string loop, the double warp threads will be parallel rather than in a zigzag arrangement.

2 / A shuttle made from a toothbrush handle

Tie knots in the warp threads as more warp is needed to cover the entire surface of the board with double vertical warps. The ends of the knots can be hidden in the web.

The weft threads are carried back and forth either with a yarn needle or with a sharpened toothbrush handle. (See Illustration 2.) These little "needle-shuttles" can be very useful for a variety of weaving. They are made by break-

ing off a discarded toothbrush and sharpening the broken end on a file. Finish with sandpaper to a smooth, sharp point. As the weft threads move over and under, from side to side on the cardboard, it may be necessary to include the string-holding loops several times, especially if the fabric is to be a solidly woven piece. (See Illustration 3.)

If you are using odd scraps of harmonizing yarns, you will have a more balanced place mat if you weave at both ends of the loom. So if you start with ten rows across the loom of one color, yellow green for example, then turn the loom around and weave ten rows across of yellow-green at the other end. When the piece is finished, and a row of binding in a matching color has been added across the ends, the cardboard loom is turned over and the binding strings are all cut from the back. The finished piece of fabric can then be lifted off the cardboard. (See Illustration 4.)

Various techniques may be used to give variety to the weave. It might be found interesting to use the cardboard loom for weaving a wall hanging with a see-through background—with various shapes woven in solid. (See Illustration 5.) If this method is used, a steam pressing on the cardboard before the bindings are clipped will help hold the threads in their position.

3 / Starting the weaving

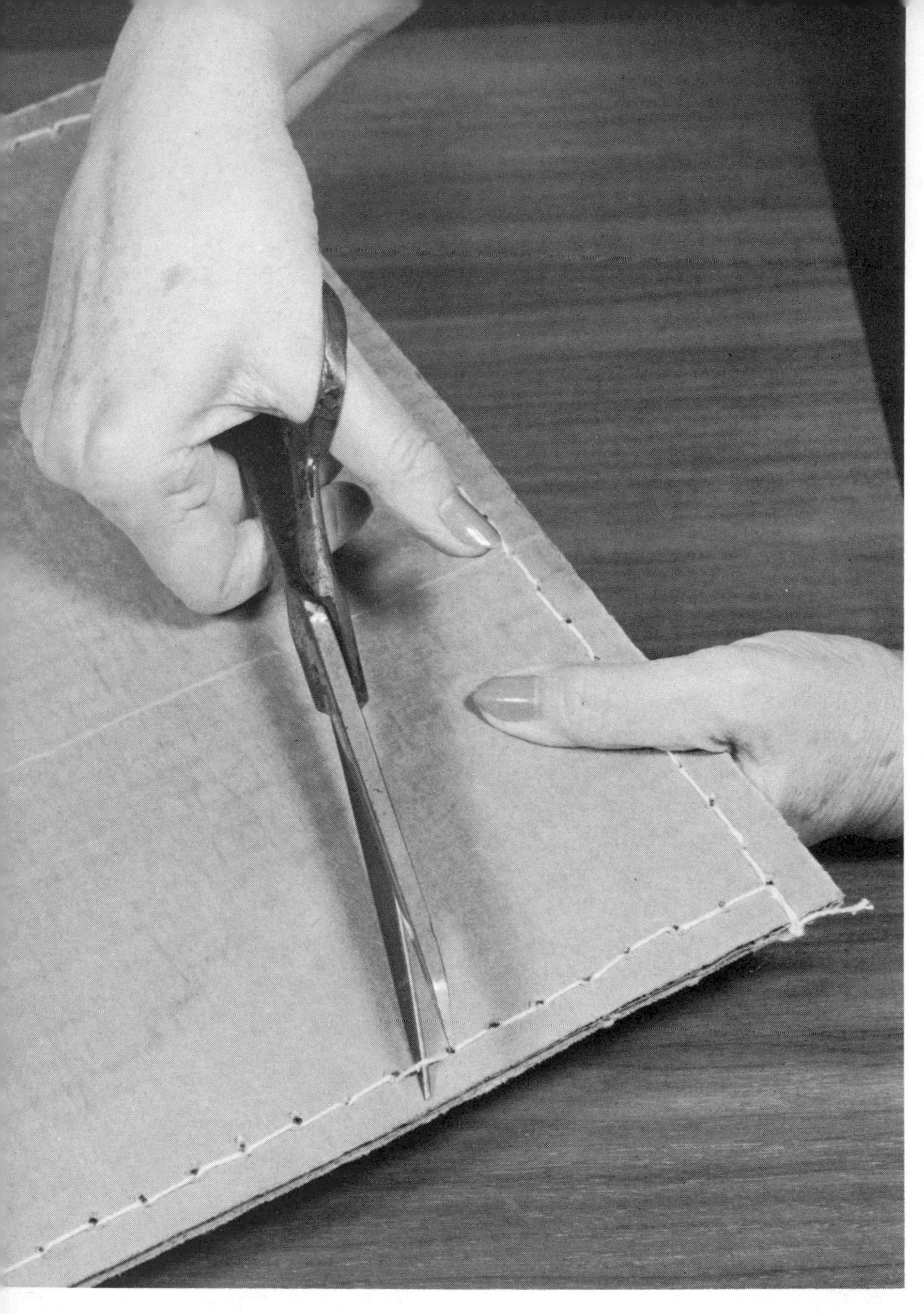

4 / Cutting the binding threads on the back of the loom

5 / Open-weave background

2

Card Weaving

The materials needed for card weaving are very simple. Select unmarred cardboard and cut it into pieces approximately 1½-by-3 inches. The number of cards cut will determine the width of the band or braid. A beginner will find four cards best as an introduction to the method.

Find the exact center of each card by drawing diagonal lines across each one. Punch a hole in the center of each of the four cards. A paper punch may be used, or a leather punch. The hole should be about ⅛ to ¼ inch in diameter.

Four warp threads are threaded individually through the cards to make one shed. A rather strong heavy thread is recommended, such as wool carpet yarn, in a single bright color until the weaver understands the method. Five warp threads in a contrasting color are used between the cards and on the edges of the warp. A suggested length of warp is 2 yards. Pimento red and off-white are a good color combination.

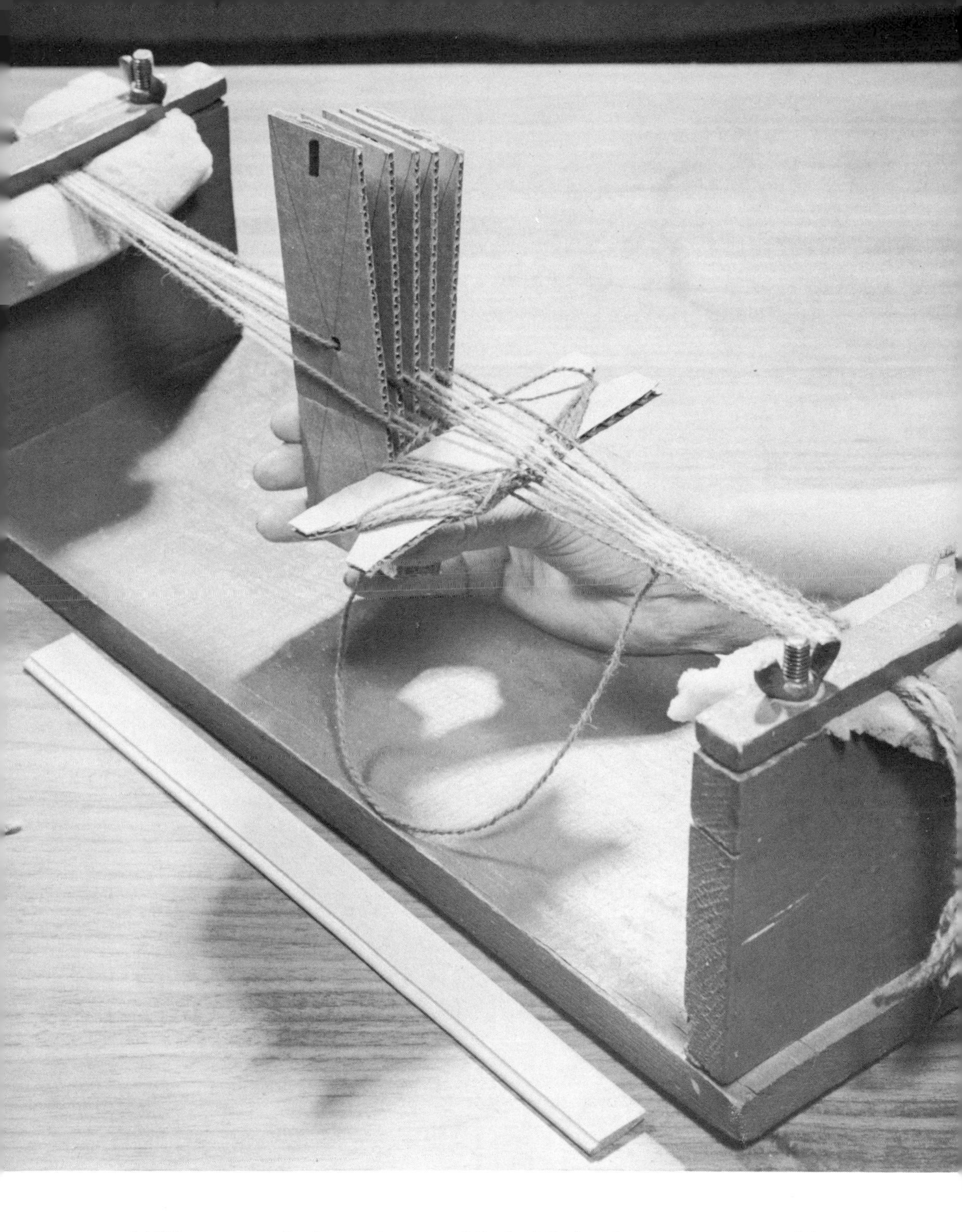

6 / Warp stretched on a frame with shuttle in place

The two-color warp must be stretched taut. All nine threads may be tied together in a knot and the knot put inside a closed drawer for a quick way to keep the warp taut. The other end of the 2-yard warp may be secured to the weaver's belt where it can be kept tightly stretched. The warp should read red, white, red, white, red, white, red, white, red. And a small cardboard shuttle should be wound with the red thread for the weft so that the selvage edges of the strap or belt will be red.

By pushing down on the four cards, all at the same time, the weaver will discover that the top shed is all red. Then by pushing up on the four cards at the same time, the shed will be all white. The cards should be moved in a rocking motion to allow the threads of the warp to move easily between the cards, keeping the tension on the warp comfortably easy. (See Illustration 6.)

Pass the shuttle through the alternating sheds from left to right, beating the weft down with a ruler.

These narrow bands make sturdy bag handles, belts, braids, and trimmings. Card weaving may also be used as a heading for fringes by inserting pre-cut lengths of yarn and allowing them to extend on one side of the band.

7 / Finished belt in simple card weaving

3

Pocket Weaving

Pocket weaving is a term used to describe weaving around and around a piece of cardboard. A 5- or 6-inch piece of cardboard will make a pocket suitable for a pincushion, while a piece of cardboard measuring 12-by-12 inches might be used for a shaggy sofa pillow. Other uses for pocket weaving are a small charge-plate holder or a case for eyeglasses. Or this type of weaving can be used for a rectangular handbag with a zipper top.

First determine the size of the pocket you want to weave, and cut the cardboard to that size, say an 8-by-12-inch bag. The best way to cut the cardboard is to hold a serrated knife blade on the pencil line rather close to a table edge, and use the knife like a saw, cutting up and down right beside the edge of the table.

Mark the cardboard with a pencil line, then cut. Then, along the side of the cardboard where you wish to place the opening or the zipper, make a row of dots with a pencil, just ½ inch apart. These dots show where to punch the holes. They can be punched through the cardboard with a fine wire nail. Be sure the holes are ½ inch from the edge of the cardboard.

Now, with a darning needle and a length of white string or carpet warp, sew in and out through the holes, first tying the white string securely at the edge. Then turn the cardboard over and sew along the row of holes as before so that each ½-inch space has white string stretched to receive and hold the warp threads.

Select pleasing colors in heavy yarns for the warp and, with a blunt yarn needle, tie the end securely into the first string loop on the left-hand side of the cardboard. Take the yarn down around the cardboard and up the other side into the corresponding loop on the back of the cardboard. Then carry the yarn down around the bottom of the cardboard and up the front side again and through the second loop. Continue in this way to wind the warp onto both sides of the cardboard. Be sure no warp threads are taken up over the top of the cardboard.

Tie on additional lengths of warp threads with a square knot, as the knots will be covered with the weft threads. When the warping is finished, it will lie in vertical lines on both sides of the cardboard, back and front, with the ½ inch of unused cardboard at the top. (See Illustration 8.)

For the weft, select harmonious colors of heavy thread or yarns that will pass easily through the large eye of the needle or the hole in the end of a shuttle made from a

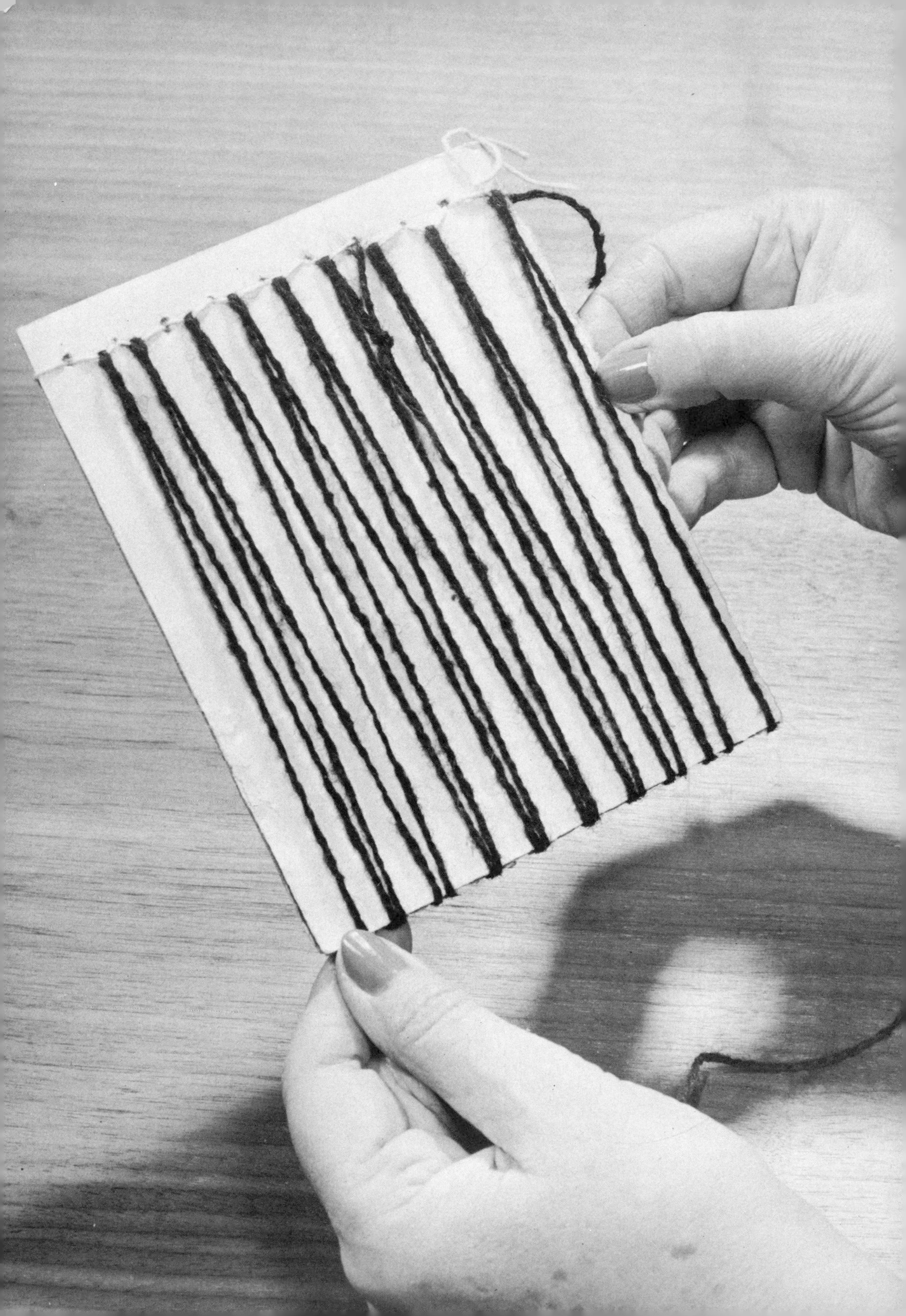

toothbrush handle which has been filed to a point. Begin weaving over and under across the warp threads beginning close to the white string binding. Instead of weaving back and forth across the cardboard, continue on around the other side of the cardboard, thus making a circle of weft thread. Continue around and around the purse or pocket, joining new weft threads when necessary by overlapping the ends and combining colors and textures as desired. Groups of threads may be used as weft. Many types of yarns such as chenilles or looped yarns will add to the originality of the bag.

A coarse-tooth comb may be used to pack the weft threads down, thus making a firmer fabric.

When the bag is completely woven, and all the warp threads are covered, cut the white string binding that holds the bag to the cardboard and slip out the cardboard.

Line the bag with a satin lining of harmonious color, sew in a zipper and add a yarn tassel for a handle. A straw or raffia bag for summer makes a good project and can be made in colors to harmonize with summer outfits.

Heavy cotton yarns such as rug yarns may be used to weave potholders, and wool knitting yarns may be woven into interesting sofa pillows with the pocket type of weaving.

8 / Warping a pocket loom

Pocket weaving makes a very desirable project for bed patients as the loom is neither cumbersome nor heavy. And the myriad of beautiful colors in yarns makes it a pleasant pastime.

One of the most effective bags made in this style was of brown wool, orange mohair loop, tan chenille, beige velvet ribbon, off-white knitting worsted, and tassels of brown yarn tied into the warp.

One good method for obtaining variety in weaving is to select a variety of threads: take

a heavy thread
a thin thread
a shiny thread
a smooth thread
a dull thread
a rough thread.

A very interesting result may be created, either with colors in the above selection, or using all one color in these varieties. In other words, thick, thin, shiny, dull, smooth and rough, a good rule to follow for more textured fabric.

9 / Weaving around and around on a pocket loom

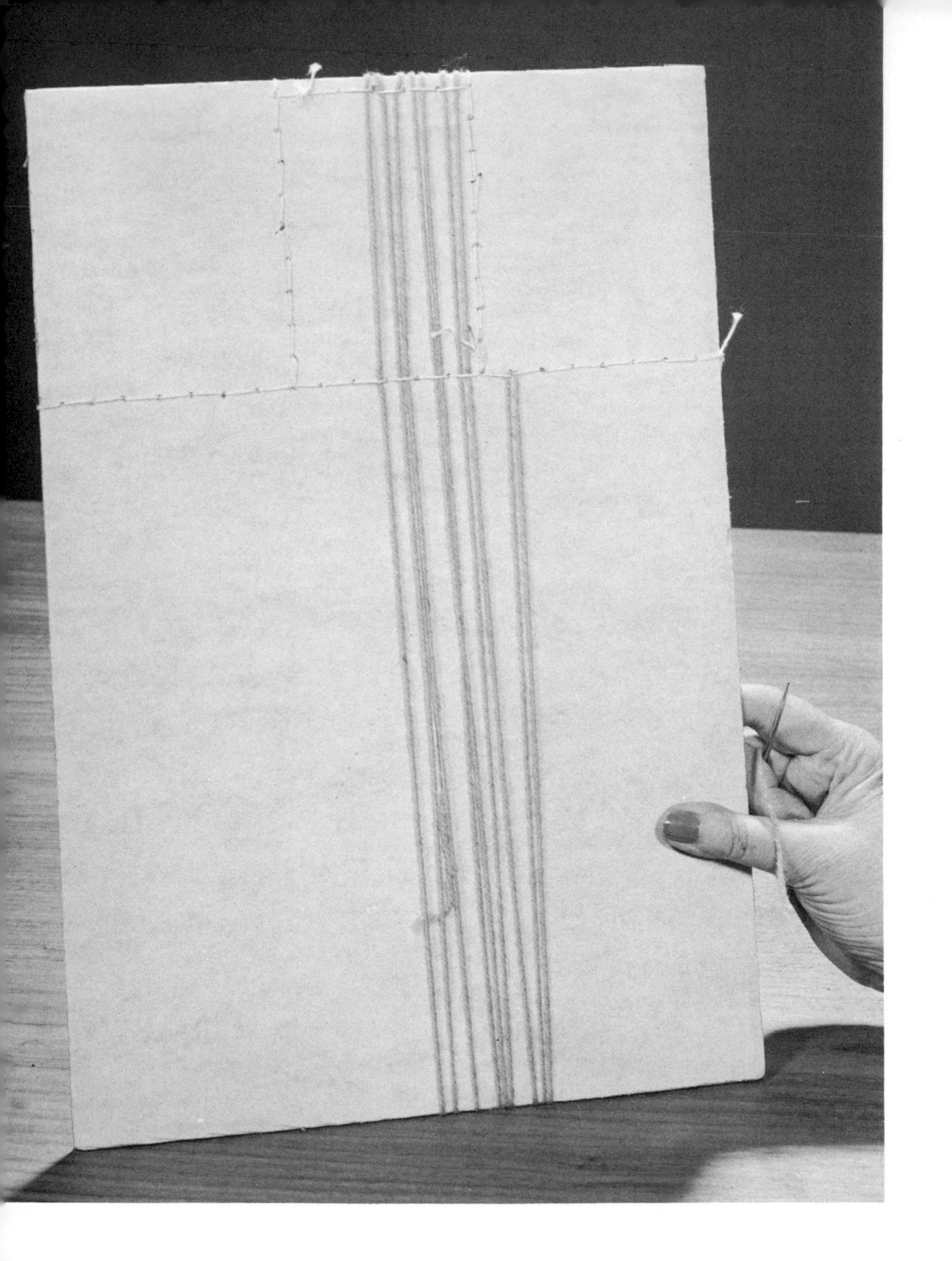

10 / Beginning the warp of a one-piece bag with handle

4

Weaving a Bag with a Handle

After working on some pocket weaving projects, it is fun to try the next step in cardboard weaving—a bag with a handle all in one.

By using a taller piece of cardboard, and taking the warp threads up over the center of the top of the cardboard, a bag can be woven all in one piece, including the handle.

First decide on the size of the bag and length of handle and, with a ruler and pencil, sketch the shape of the bag on the flat cardboard. The bag part of the weaving will be done in pocket style, with the weft threads weaving around and around the cardboard. However, after the pocket is woven, the same type of weaving is continued back and forth on the handle, catching each weft thread in the binding to hold it in place.

To make a bag which measures 12-by-12 inches you will need a piece of cardboard 12 inches wide but 16 inches high to allow for the handle. The weaving will begin very much like pocket weaving. Measure across the cardboard at the 12-inch line, mark and punch holes across it every ½ inch, and, with a darning needle and white string or carpet warp, sew through every hole once across the front and back, as with the pocket loom.

Then mark a 4-inch area up through the center of the cardboard and punch ½-inch holes along the two lines. Also punch holes and put a binding string across the handle panel ½-inch down from the top of the cardboard. These binding strings may be entered again and again with the weaving shuttle to keep the selvages straight.

Care must be taken to keep the cardboard absolutely straight and unbent during the weaving, as the warp threads in all cardboard weaving must be kept comfortably taut.

Tie the first warp thread at the left-hand binding string, then carry it down around the bottom of the cardboard and up the other side to the corresponding binding string, then back around the cardboard and catch through the next binding string, and continue in this manner, adding yarn when necessary with a square knot.

When the warp reaches the center panel for the handle, take the yarn all around the cardboard, catching through all the binding threads to hold it in place. Thus the warp threads swing under the cardboard to make a pocket, but swing over, down, and around when they are incorporated into the handle. (See Illustration 10.)

The shuttle used to carry the weft thread may be a large-eye yarn needle or a sharpened toothbrush handle. Single threads may be used but unusual effects may be gained by combining several colors on the shuttle for the weft. The weaving begins as in pocket weaving, round and round the cardboard, changing colors and textures as the weaver desires. The same type of weaving continues on the handle, but must be woven back and forth in the normal style, continuing right over the top of the cardboard and meeting the top of the bag on the other side.

When the weaving is finished and well-packed, the fabric is removed from the cardboard by carefully cutting the white string bindings and slipping the cardboard out of the bag. It may be necessary to cut the cardboard to facilitate taking it out. The bag can be fitted with a lining. And sheets of buckram for stiffening can be cut to fit the sides between the lining and the bag.

One very effective bag was made with shades of soft green wool yarns with olive green, gray-green, and nile green combined on the shuttle or needle for the weft. The bag was lined with olive-green satin.

Another was a small evening bag woven of shiny pink rayon with pearls strung on the weft thread at intervals throughout the weaving. The bag was lined with pink satin with a snap fastener to hold it together.

5

Weaving a Belt on One Piece of Cardboard

Although the preparation of the strip of cardboard takes quite a bit of time, the woven belt is well worth the time consumed. Take a piece of smooth cardboard about 3 inches wide and 20 inches long.

The piece must be half the waist measurement desired for the belt. A considerably longer piece should be used for a belt to be tied or looped.

Mark, with pencil and ruler, a line all around the piece, on one side only, just ½ inch from the outside edge. Along this line mark dots for nail holes ½ inch apart.

Sew through the holes with twine or carpet warp, beginning with a tied knot and continuing all around the piece, making two trips, so that there is a binding loop every ½ inch all around the cardboard.

The above method is the same as used on the place mat type of binding. The purpose of the binding is just to hold the threads, both warp and weft, in place during the weaving and to insure a good selvage.

Select rather heavy warp yarns in a pleasing color combination. Slip the first warp thread through the first binding loop, take it up over the end of the cardboard, catching in both the bindings at the top, and down through the first matching binding on the other side of the cardboard, and tie it in a knot, thus entirely circling the loom.

These warp threads may be tied together and cut off. Proceed to warp the belt loom in the above fashion. The warp yarns will be mostly covered by the weft colors, so it makes little difference what color is chosen. There will be seven or more heavy warp threads, according to the width of the belt.

The weft threads are woven back and forth on one side of the cardboard, using the binding cords along the edge to keep the selvage straight. (See Illustration 11.) It may be necessary to use the same binding loop several times in order to keep the weft threads weaving straight across the belt.

For a shuttle to carry the threads back and forth across such a short distance, a yarn needle will be found to be very satisfactory. When new lengths of wefts are to be joined, you may overlap the ends underneath.

If a more solid weave is desired, the binding threads may be spaced closer together. In fact, some very effective belts have been made with 1/4-inch or even 1/8-inch spaces left between the holes for the binder string.

To remove the belt when finished, the binding strings are carefully cut, the white strings removed, and the belt lifted in one piece from the cardboard. It may be finished at the ends in a number of different ways. One effective finish is to tie in rather long fringes at each end, with a snitch knot, fastening the belt with a single loop.

Another very interesting effect was obtained by covering two hollow flat rings, about 2 inches in diameter and about ½ inch wide, with harmonizing colors of yarn, wrapping around and around the rings so as to cover them completely. The rings were cut from plastic bottles, which cut very easily with scissors. Two lids of the right size were placed on flat pieces of the plastic bottle, drawn around with a sharp pencil point and cut with scissors. When the rings are attached to the ends of the belt, they can be held together by a looped cord which matches the colors in the belt.

11 / Weaving a wide belt with several weft yarns in the same binding loops

6

Weaving a Purse with a Flap

After a weaver has tried both flat weaving on cardboard, in which the weft threads are taken back and forth from left to right to make a fabric, and also the pocket type weaving, in which the weft is taken around and around the cardboard to double the fabric, he is then ready to try the two procedures together on one piece of cardboard.

The body of the purse is woven pocket style, round and round using both sides of the cardboard. The flap is a continuation of the weaving on one side only, to produce a piece of fabric which is folded down over the pocket, envelope style.

To make a purse 9-by-12 inches, select a smooth piece of corrugated cardboard. The piece will have to be 14-by-12 inches to make a finished purse with a flap. Measure with a ruler, and put a line around the cardboard ½ inch from the edge on all four sides. Then draw another line just 9 inches above one end. Along all these lines mark dots ½ inch apart and punch holes in the cardboard with a sharp nail. When the holes are all punched, take a darning needle and white cotton string or carpet warp and put a binding thread all around the edge and through the center line, making two sewings so that both sides of the cardboard will have binding threads to hold the fabric. Be sure all the bindings are securely tied, as the warp threads will put a strain on the bindings.

For a winter bag select heavy wool yarns. With a yarn needle and a 2-yard length of heavy yarn, tie the end to the middle binding cord at one edge and carry the yarn down around the cardboard and all the way up to the top on the other side of the cardboard. Then catch the yarn in the binding loop next to the one just used and bring the yarn down around the bottom of the cardboard and up to the center line. Continue the process, putting on the warp threads to make a pocket type of weaving at the bottom of the purse and a single layer of weaving for the flap. (See Illustration 12.)

As the weaving progresses, the weft may be packed down tightly with a coarse-tooth comb. The ends of the thread in the needle or shuttle must be overlapped when joining a new thread. Knots in the warp should not be cut too short but rather left long so that they will be covered by the weft. Unusual effects are gained by inserting in the weft bits of chiffon, velvet, or ribbon. Gold and silver metallic threads create a rich effect.

When the pocket and flap are completely woven, remove the bag from the cardboard by cutting the white

binding cords. The cardboard will slip out of the bag easily. Cut a lining and insert it by hand sewing. A large loop and button may be used to keep the flap closed or a snap fastener can be sewn to the lining. This type of bag may be made with a long shoulder handle of finger weaving, finger looping, spool weaving, or one-hole cardboard weaving to add another technique.

12 / A purse with a flap

7

Weaving a Round Mat on Cardboard

There is a fascination to weaving in the round. Almost everyone, no matter what his age, is caught up by the idea of producing a piece of fabric round in shape.

Select a piece of cardboard and a plate or tray or compass of the right size. Pick a nail for the holes, a darning needle with white string for the binding, a yarn needle or shuttle made from a sharpened toothbrush handle, or a whittled wooden bodkin, and you are ready to begin.

Draw a large circle with the help of a plate or tray, about 10 or 12 inches in diameter. Holding the cardboard securely down on a table, cut on the line with a serrated steak knife.

Draw a line ½ inch from the edge of the circle and mark dots ½ inch apart on the line. With the sharp nail punch a hole on each dot. Thread the darning needle with white cotton string or carpet warp and sew a binding thread around the cardboard, going around twice so that the thread is stretched across every ½-inch space.

Select heavy yarns—rayon, cotton, wool—or any available fiber, and thread a 2-yard length into a yarn needle. Slip through one loop, carry thread across the circle on a true diameter, and tie a knot in the center of the circle to mark it. Proceed around the binder loops in a clockwise motion, being sure that each thread returns to the center of the cardboard circle. (See Illustration 13.) This warps the mat in the manner of spokes on a wheel.

Begin to weave around the center of the circle, pulling the yarn tight into a small circle at the center of the cardboard. The weaving can be done by using single spokes or double spokes. As the thread is used in the bodkin, needle, or shuttle, overlap ends of the new thread with the end of the used thread. (See Illustration 14.)

After circling the spokes once it may be noticed that an even number of spokes will not weave correctly in a round-and-round way, so correct the weaving line as is necessary by slipping under two loops instead of one.

When warping the cardboard, you will find that an uneven number of spokes is to be desired, so an extra spoke may be inserted while warping the mat.

Be sure to select colors wisely, perhaps using gradations of one or two colors such as dark green, blue green, nile green, ice green, henna, butterscotch, beige, and so on for a mat to place under a lamp.

Vary the weft rings in size by changing the length of yarn used in the shuttle or needle. Try to work for great variety of color and size in the rings.

13 / Warping a round mat

14 / Weaving a round mat

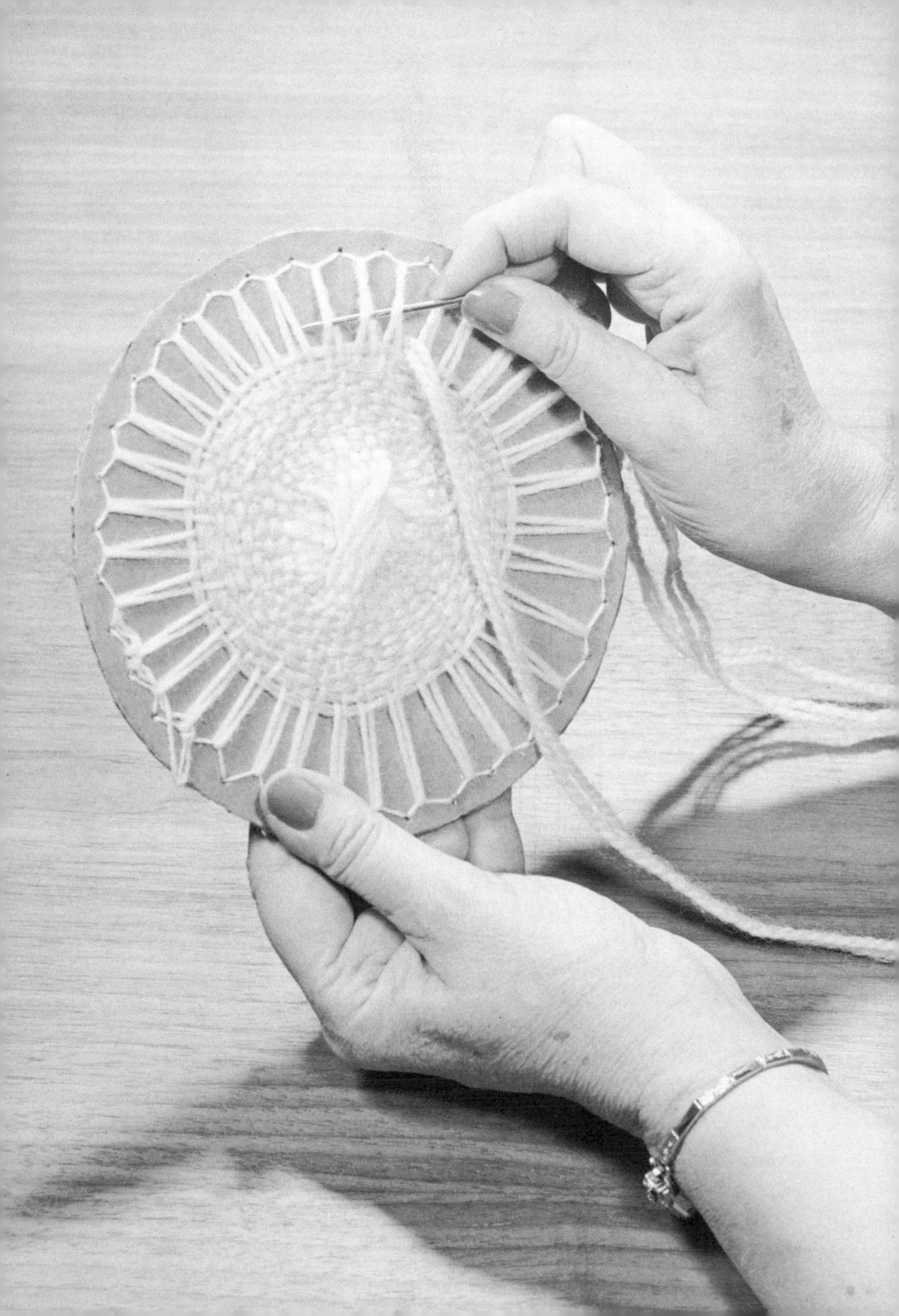

When the weaving is finished, steam press the mat and remove it from the cardboard by cutting all the white carpet warp strings from the cardboard. Before cutting the mat loose, check each spoke to be sure there is a weft thread going under and over each one.

An interesting finish is to tie in fringes of 3-inch lengths of yarn at each warp spoke. Round mats may be used in many different ways, such as pockets on a skirt, under lamps or vases, or in pairs laced together to form a bag or purse.

One interesting use of a piece of large round weaving was a poncho, with a slit cut through the center after first machine-stitching to prevent unraveling, and then bound with tape to make a hole for the head. Heavy fringes added at the edge made a beautiful finish.

The same type of weaving can be done on a piece of ¼-inch plywood with finishing nails to hold the warp in a circle for a bath mat or rug. With this method, as the weaving progresses and the spokes become farther and farther apart, additional spokes can be tied into the weft yarns to keep the weaving more solid.

When making a rug by this method, heavy cotton roving yarns should be used to give strength and body to the rug. Carpet rags could also be chosen and, when these are used, it is not necessary to thread them into a needle or bodkin. Just finger weave the weft rags, overlapping the ends when necessary.

8

Weaving a Scarf or Stole on Cardboard

Select a piece of unmarred cardboard as wide and just half as long as you desire the scarf to be.

Put a row of ½-inch holes at each end of the cardboard. The warp will be taken over the top of the cardboard and down the other side, thus making the scarf twice as long as the size of the cardboard.

Using both sides of the cardboard keeps the loom small and very easy to handle. For a scarf 8 inches wide and 30 inches long, select a piece of cardboard 8 inches by 15 inches. With a needle and white cotton string or carpet warp, sew the binding threads at both ends only of the cardboard.

This type of weaving lends itself to the use of various bits of scrap wool yarns. Mohair, angora, weaving wool used in bundles, metallics, loops, handspuns; in fact, many varieties of yarns may be used for both warp and weft.

One interesting scarf was made with odds and ends of

white and off-white yarns in a variety of dulls, loops, shiny yarns, all in creamy colors for the warp. The entire weft was woven with white orlon knitting worsted.

The warping of the loom is very similar to that of place mat weaving. The first warp thread is tied in the first string loop, carried up to the other end of the cardboard, through a loop on the front and also a loop on the back and down on the back of the cardboard to the first corresponding loop on the back of the cardboard. The second thread continues in the second binder loop, and so on until both sides of the cardboard are covered with the warp yarn.

The weft threads are carried back and forth across the warp threads. Care must be taken not to pull in the side selvages. A yarn needle, bodkin, or sharpened toothbrush handle may be used as a shuttle.

The weaving continues up one face of the cardboard and down the other side, thus making the scarf twice as long as the cardboard.

Various techniques in the weaving may be used for the scarf. One suggestion would be many different types of woolen or orlon yarns in the same color or closely related colors. The knotting-in of various bits of yarn adds an interesting, three-dimensional effect to the scarf.

If the weaver finds the weft threads are pulling in toward the center, he might punch holes along the sides of the cardboard and put binder cords in to hold the side edges even, as in Illustration 11.

Twelve-inch lengths of yarn may be cut and tied onto

the scarf ends as groups or bundles to make a heavy fringe. The fringe will, of course, add to the length of the scarf and also give it a decorative touch. The fringe should be added after the scarf has been released from the cardboard by clipping the binding cords.

9

Wrapping a Mat on Cardboard

There are some wrapping techniques which, although they are not really classified as weaving—since they are done with a continuous thread, rather than with many interlacing warp and weft threads—nevertheless make attractive articles.

One such technique involves a hot dish mat wrapped with yarns, in which the cardboard inside the mat is not removed, but acts as insulation.

To make a wrapped mat, select yarns similar in weight, either cottons, or wools, or rayons in bright, sharp colors. Cut a square of cardboard which measures 6 inches. Be sure the cardboard is flat and unblemished. Cut out a square in the center of the piece which measures 4 inches. Cut and measure accurately, using a ruler, pencil, and serrated steak knife. By cutting out the center of the original 6-inch square, a shape not unlike a frame remains.

Select the first color and tie it around one side of the

frame next to the corner. Slip the ball of yarn through the center hole and wrap around the frame directly across the square. Make a quarter turn of the cardboard and place a strand around the same corner. Be sure that there are two wrapped threads on each corner, going both ways, before carrying the thread across the square. (See the white threads in Illustration 15.) This method completely covers the cardboard on both sides. The exposed corners of the mat will later be covered with 1-inch squares of felt in a harmonizing color.

When the same number of threads has been wrapped on all four corners, tie on the next color with a square knot and continue to wrap. Vary the number of times the colors are changed so as to give variety in color arrangement. The ends of the knots where new colors are added may be inserted between the cardboard and the wrapping.

When the mat is as full of threads as is comfortable or possible to wind, cut the end of the thread and fasten down with glue. Then glue eight squares of felt on the eight corners of exposed cardboard. (See Illustration 16.)

These decorative mats may be used in a great many ways.

Another interesting wrapping technique may be done on wooden lollipop sticks, or flat, identical wooden sticks. The wrapping can be done like weaving, except that the sticks are used as a warp and therefore remain in the mat. Select a variety of interesting colors of cotton, wool, or rayon threads, not necessarily the same in size or texture. The color combinations must be pleasing. Select any

15 / Wrapping a hot dish mat

16 / A finished mat with felt corners in the background

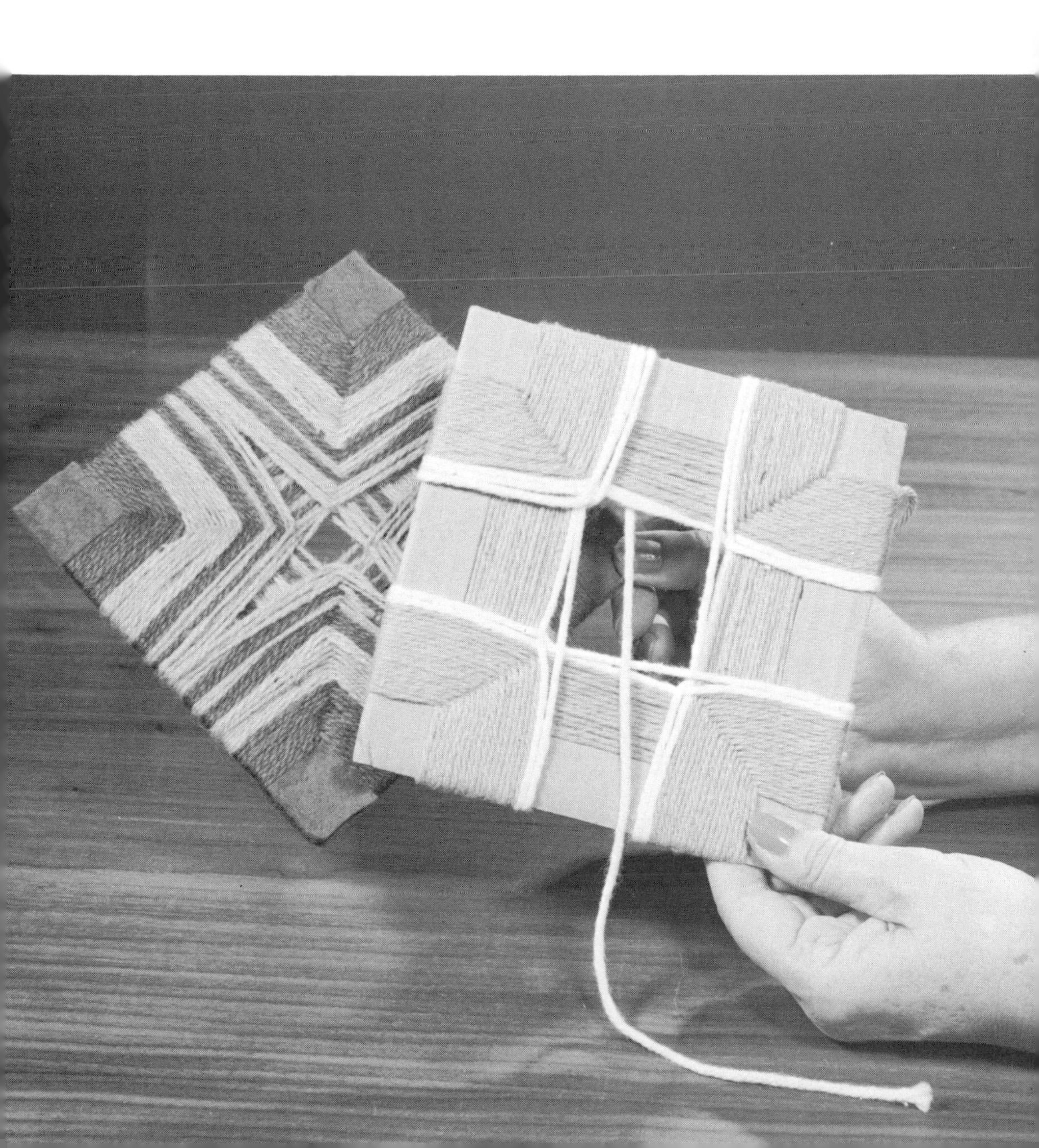

number of sticks which will make a square surface, and, holding them in place on a table edge, tie on the first thread and weave it across all the sticks. At the last stick, turn and weave back across all the sticks, pulling them into a straight formation. When the sticks are all covered with the wrapping, or, really, the weft colors are on the sticks as warp, the end of the last thread can be fastened down to the sticks with glue.

For lack of a better name, these little mats might be called wrapped stick mats. A variety of types of thread adds to the beauty of the piece. One might use chenille or flake cotton or fine shiny rayons. Since all of the stick, except ½ inch at each end, will be covered with the weft threads, many more turns across the warp sticks will be necessary if fine threads are used. After the first few weft threads are put in place, the sticks will hold their formation until all are covered (or all except the last ½ inch). Vinyl sticks, from discarded matchstick blinds, may be cut and used in this manner.

Another interesting use of sticks wrapped with yarns or threads is the wrapped cross, commonly called "God's-eye." These were supposedly made by Indians to ward off evil spirits.

Fasten the yarn with a knot at the center of two crossed sticks, the first strand chosen of a bright color yarn. Holding the sticks at right angles, begin to wrap under, then

17 / Wrapping threads on crossed sticks for a "God's-eye"

around each stick, progressing clockwise around the four sticks. All of the sticks must be covered and then fastened off with glue. The effect is of a flat mat composed of concentric squares with an eye in the center. It may be hung by a corner and makes a very effective decoration. They have been used as dangles, in miniature form, for a necklace and also as Christmas tree decorations made with bright colors and metallic threads.

Bracelets in desired colors may be wrapped on rings cut from plastic soap bottles. Here again the choice of colors and types of threads or yarns determines the effectiveness of the finished wrapping.

Wrapping the vertical sides of juice cans or coffee cans makes a very simple but effective decorative technique. Both ends of a juice can are removed, then the yarns wrapped around the length of the can, and a plastic lid used to close one end of the can after it has been wrapped.

Cans wrapped around and around make simple gifts such as pencil holders that quite young children can make.

17a / A God's-eye finished with tassels

10

Weaving a Triangle Headscarf on Cardboard

This method of weaving a triangular scarf is unique, in that the entire triangle of fabric is composed of warp threads only. After the warp yarns are put on the loom, each thread is lifted in order and turned across the loom to make a weft thread.

Select a piece of cardboard 20-by-23 inches. Cut it accurately with a serrated knife. Draw a line ½ inch from the top edge and down the left side. Draw another line across the top about 3 inches below the top line so that it and the left side line make a perfect square. Then draw a diagonal line from that to the bottom of the left side.

Make dots at ½-inch intervals on the lines and punch holes through the cardboard with a wire nail. With a white string or carpet warp in a darning needle, sew all around through the holes, in and out, progressing around twice so as to make a continuous binding cord to hold the yarn.

Keep the cardboard straight and unbent during the binding process.

Select an assortment of pleasing colors in various wools, mohair, orlon, or loop threads. Slip the first color of the warp through the second top string, carry it up to the top of the loom and through the first corresponding loop directly above it. Then carry it down through the same first loop and cut it a few inches longer than the cardboard. This helps keep the warp threads from pulling out of the string loops. If the yarns chosen are fine in gauge, they may be used in groups or bunches. When the warp threads are suspended all across the loom, they will be held in place by the two parallel lines of binding cords.

Now for the fun. Use a smooth, sharpened toothbrush handle or a lacing bodkin or a large blunt yarn needle, and thread the first group of warp. Weave over and under across the loom slipping through the first loop on the diagonal. This turns the warp thread at a right angle and takes it across all the other warp threads. Allow the ends to extend and hang out over the edge of the cardboard.

Pull out the second warp, or bundle, or group of yarns in the second binding cord and thread the loose ends in the bodkin. Slip the warp threads through the next lower loop on the diagonal line, and continue to weave across the loom. (See Illustration 18.) After the first two the weaver will quickly see that the warp threads become the weft threads—each one becoming shorter and shorter until very little space remains to be covered by the last weft thread.

Before removing the scarf from the cardboard, a heavy yarn overcast on all the edges helps to hold the scarf in shape. Steam-pressing the scarf before removing it from the cardboard will also help to hold the shape. An easy way to remove the scarf from the cardboard is to turn the board over and cut all the binding cords. This allows the triangular piece of weaving to fall off the board.

It will be noticed that the fringes which were the original warp ends at the bottom of the loom are now along one side of the triangle. Corresponding fringes may be tied in along the other side of the triangle if desired.

Another variation of triangle weaving might be a large plaid shawl for which it would be necessary to prepare a much larger square of cardboard since only half the square becomes the size of the triangular piece of fabric.

18 / Weaving across the loom for a triangular headscarf

11

Weaving a Collar on Cardboard

A necklace or collar makes an interesting fashion item to add an individual touch to a simple dress. This same method of weaving a circular flat band may be used to weave a yoke for a dress or sweater.

The method of weaving may vary with the use, but the one described here is for a necklace or collar, not fastened to the dress, but worn over it.

Draw two circles, one inside the other, with the help of plates on a smooth, flat sheet of cardboard. The space between the two circles will serve as the loom for the collar or necklace, so the size may be judged accordingly.

Mark ½-inch dots around both penciled rings. Select colors of yarns or metallic threads to harmonize with the dress for which the necklace is intended. Tie the binding cord into two holes and with a darning needle and binding cord of carpet warp, sew around both rings twice, as in other types of cardboard weaving.

Begin the warping with a large darning needle and the desired colors of yarns, sewing from one circle to another, lacing the warp back and forth, as nearly straight across the circles as possible. (See Illustration 19.)

Now mark an opening line, over which none of the weft threads will pass. This opening line will serve as a turning point for the weft threads. Weave around the neck part of the necklace to the line, then turn, and weave back, so that the collar or necklace can be tied around the neck or fastened with a hook.

By changing the colors of the weft, weaving around, over, and under the warp spokes, stripes will appear to go around the neck. However, an interesting collar can be made by weaving tabs, or individual tongue-shaped areas, around the collar.

When the weaving is complete, check each area to be sure the warps are covered in order, before detaching from the cardboard brace.

Steam-pressing the flat piece before removing from the cardboard helps the collar or necklace to retain its shape. A buttonhole stitch, worked firmly around the inside circle before removing the piece from the cardboard, also helps hold the shape. A braided tie may be attached to be tied at the back of the neck, or a hook can be attached.

Various other accessories may be woven in this manner, such as pockets to be attached to a dress or a medallion to be appliquéd.

You might want to try a more elaborate type of weav-

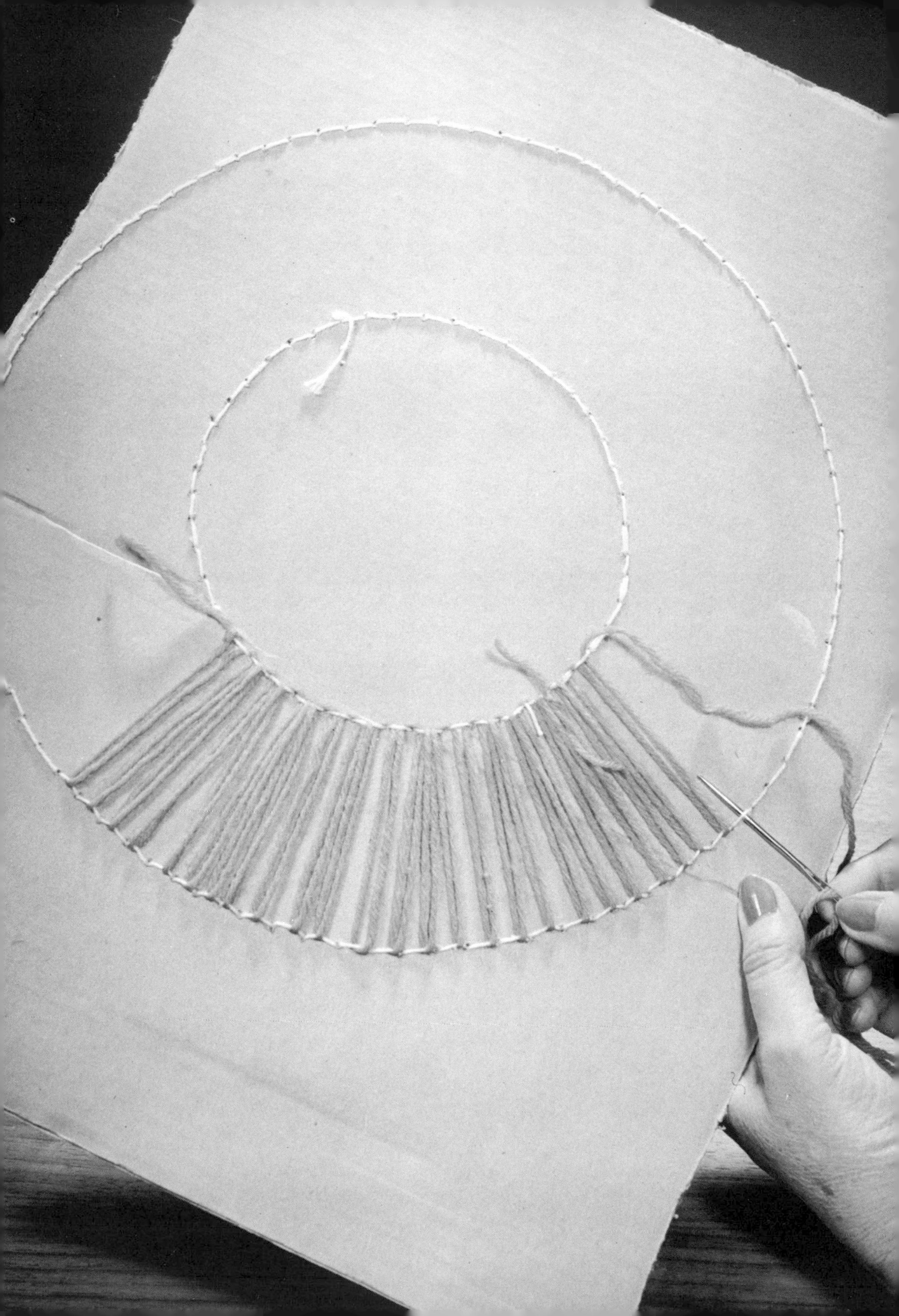

ing for clothing, say a cap woven with open spaces where the warp is pulled apart by the weft threads, or a vest made with handwoven front panels. Draw around a vest pattern on a piece of cardboard. Warp in the usual way, holding the warp threads to the board by means of lacing. Keeping the warp threads vertical, weave a variety of heavy weft threads into the vest fronts.

19 / Warping a collar

12

Weaving Fabrics of Unusual Shape on Cardboard

Now that you have progressed through this much of cardboard weaving or, at least, have read about doing it, you may be intrigued by trying some unusual shapes. You know that the cardboard is used as a stretcher for the warp and that the warp is held onto the cardboard by means of a string lacing. So why not try to warp your loom in odd shapes? This is not a new idea: in the Middle Ages the ladies in their castles were busy lace weaving on cards to make medallions.

Various shapes such as triangles, tree shapes, ovals, stars, and other flat figures may first be drawn on the cardboard in the size desired. Then the shape selected is outlined with ½-inch-apart nail holes and the darning needle lacing string put in. Simple animal shapes lend themselves to this method.

Take, for example, an oval shape measuring 18-by-6 inches. The warp threads are bound to the binding threads

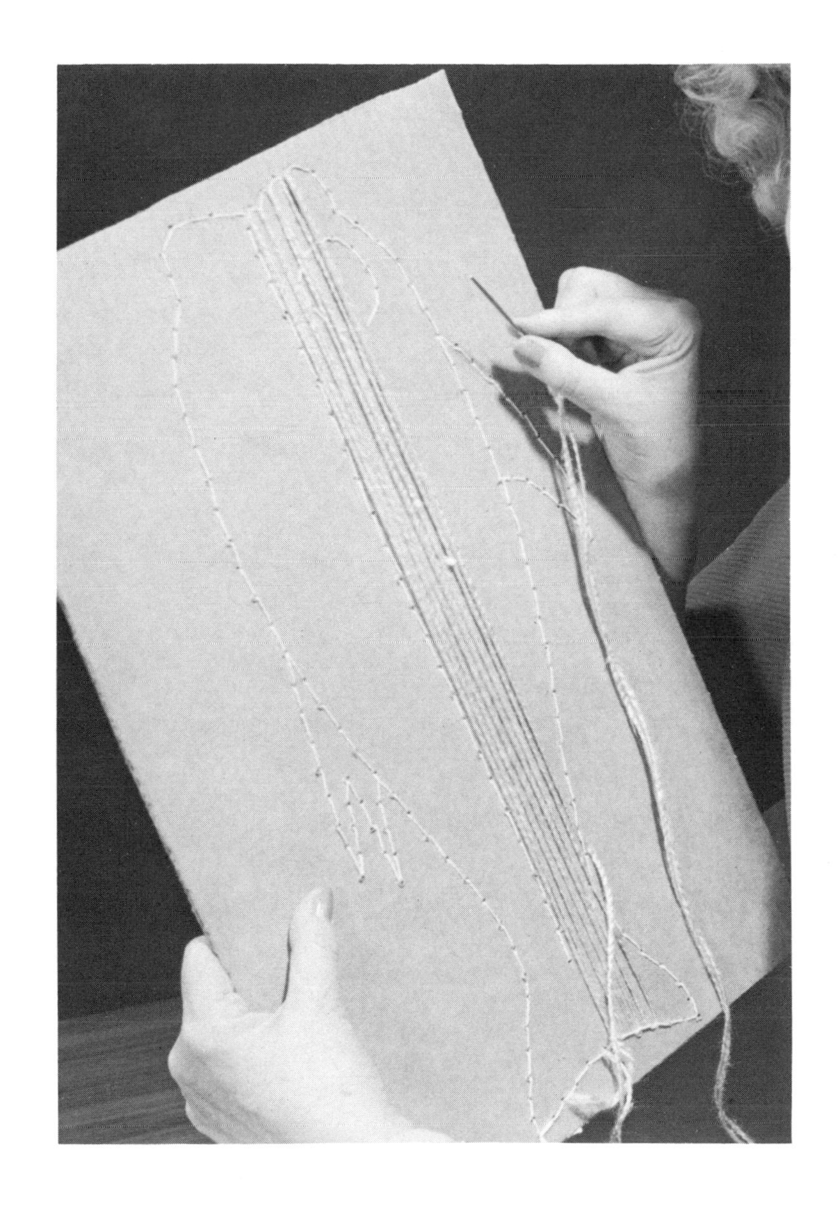

20 / A loom for a fish-shaped piece

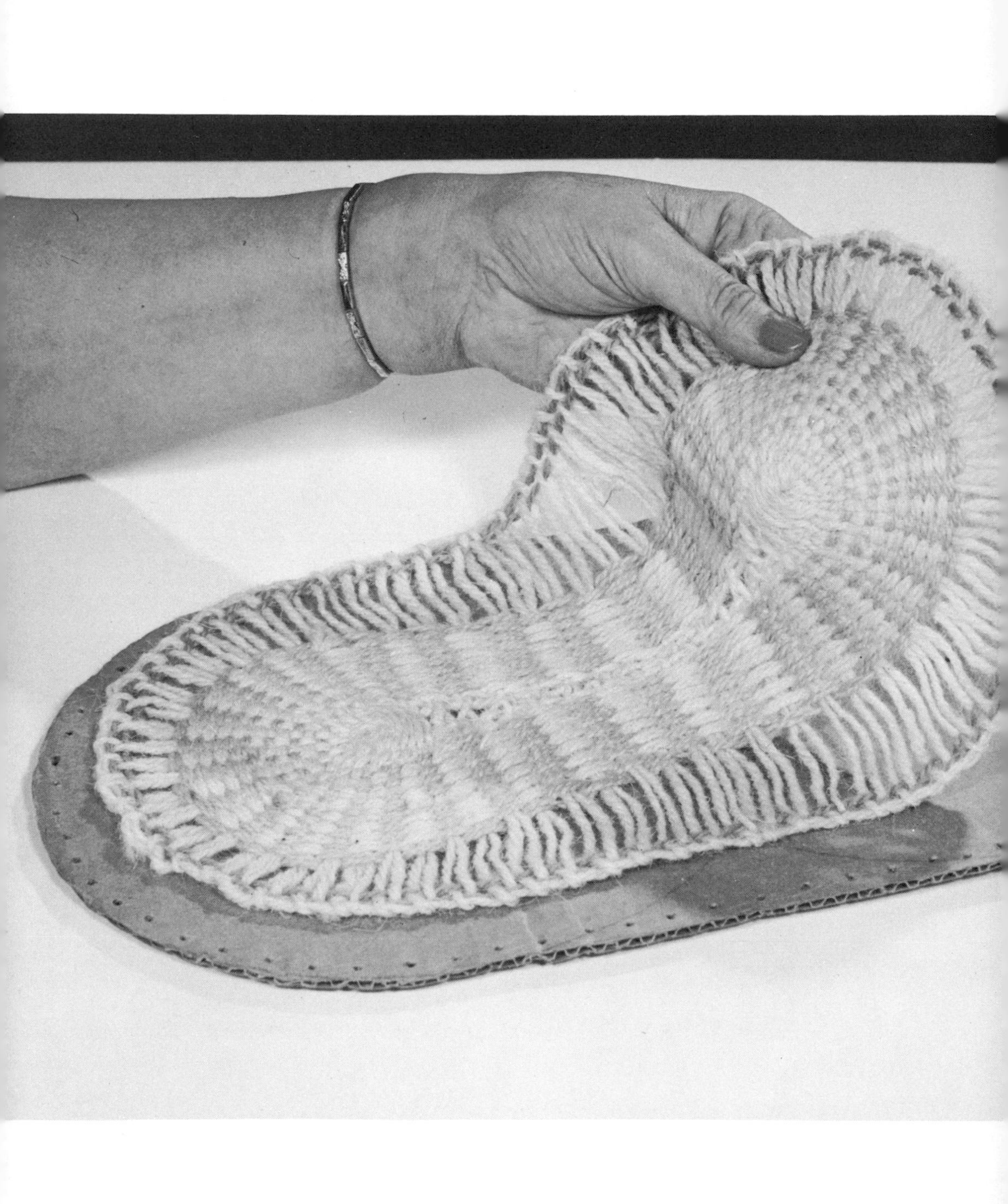

and carried back and forth across the shape. The weaving of the weft threads is done with a blunt needle.

In Illustration 21 a row of binding threads was laced down the center of the oval and the warp threads carried from the edge of the oval shape to the center line, and back to the edge. Then the weaving of the weft thread was done round and round very much as in round mat weaving.

When removing the shaped weaving from the cardboard backing, be sure to check that all the spokes or warp threads are securely anchored by the weft. It may be necessary to run an overcast stitch around the edge so that the shape will have a good selvage.

21 / Removing an oval-shaped mat from a loom

13

Weaving on Plastic Soda Straws

Although weaving on plastic soda straws can't be called weaving on cardboard, I cannot pass over a type of fabric-making which gives so much pleasure to young children. It can be carried about in a small box or pocket, requires no tools, is easy and satisfying to do, and is a delight to people from six to sixty.

First get five plastic drinking straws. Tie a large knot at the end of each strand of yarn to keep it from slipping down the straw on the inside.

Knot a string of carpet warp to the other end of the yarn to pull it through the straw. After the five straws are threaded in this way, hold the straws in the left hand with the large knots up.

The warp threads which are in each of the straws should be cut about a yard long: five yarn warps and five straws. Slip the end of the weft yarn under the left thumb and weave in and out across the little straw loom, holding the

22 / Weaving on plastic soda straws

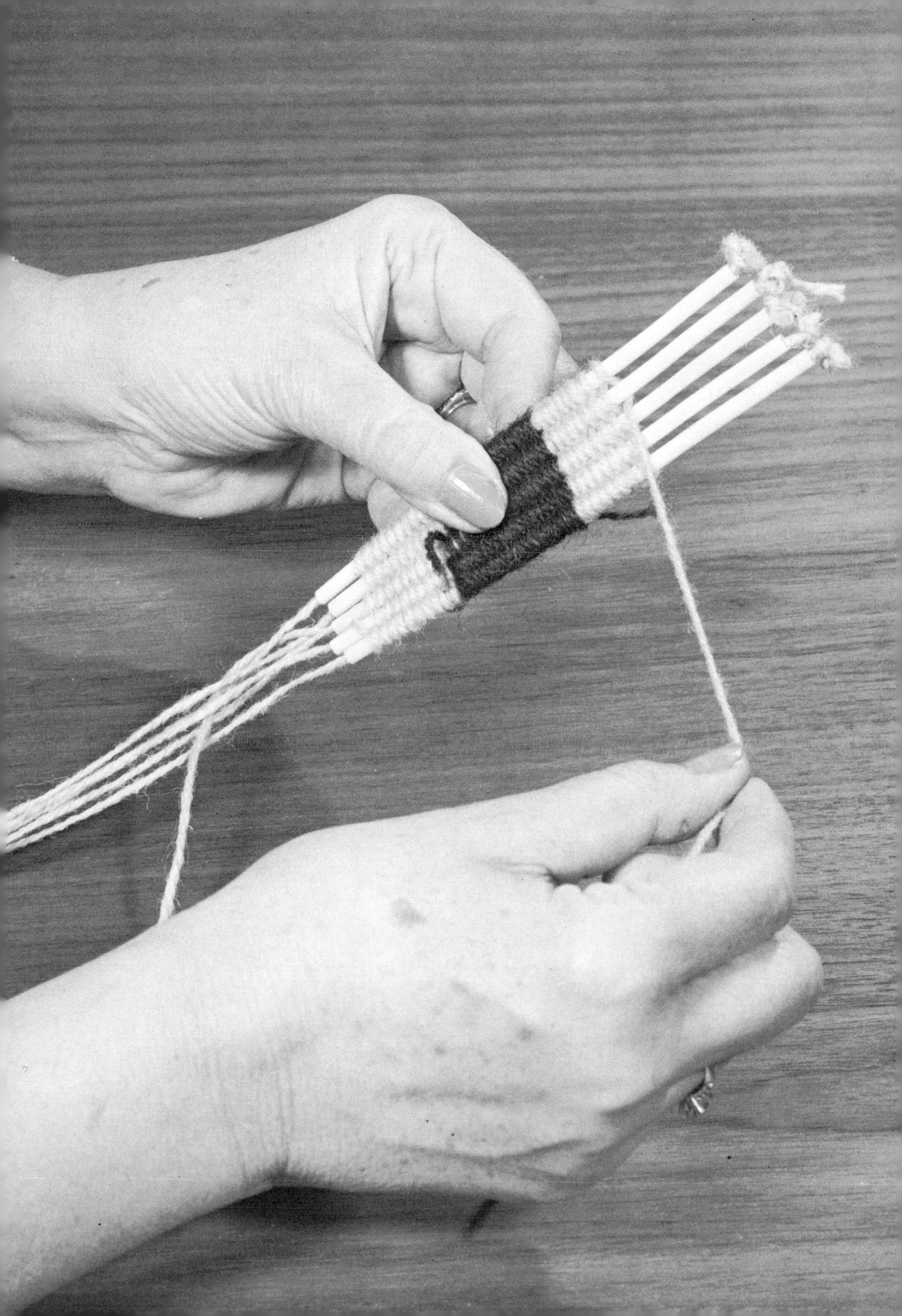

straws just close enough together to allow the weft to slip down between the straws. Many colors of wool yarn may be used, depending upon the use for the straw weaving.

Keep the fabric on the straws and twist the straws up a little as soon as it becomes necessary to have more "loom." The web or fabric works down the straws and onto the yarn all by itself.

A girl's headband or a boy's belt makes a suitable beginning project in straw weaving for a six-year-old. All he needs is a yardstick to measure his five warp threads, a large blunt needle to thread the straws, several colors of soft wool yarns, scissors (in case he wants to vary the stripes in his belt), and some help in tying five bulky knots, and, lo, he is a weaver.

Weaving on straws has several educational aspects, since the weaver must measure with a yardstick, must count the five straws, must choose harmonizing colors and cut with scissors.

Straw-weaving can be done on any number of straws, from two to as many as you can hold in your hand, and can be made more complicated if desired.

Headbands, bracelets, and belts have been very successful projects for small children.

14

Weaving on Pre-formed Cardboard

Many cardboard shapes and figures are available today in the form of discarded cartons such as salt boxes, round oats boxes, sturdy square containers, and similarly shaped cardboard.

These may be used in many ways to weave interesting containers. Some of these boxes are adapted to being left in the web of weaving to give stability to the article, but the weaver may also wish to remove the box. In that case, the cardboard container is carefully cut away.

Take an oatmeal box and carefully measure a line about 4 inches above the bottom of the box. With a serrated knife, cut the box with a sawing motion. Draw a line ½ inch below the cut top of the box, and mark dots on the line every ½ inch. Punch holes through the dots with a sharp nail and, with a darning needle and white carpet warp string, sew a binding in each hole, in and out, around twice to hold the warp.

If the entire box is to be covered, including the bottom, paint the box with a heavy coat of latex or acrylic paint in a harmonious color.

The warp thread is tied to one of the binding stitches, carried down and across the bottom of the box and up on the opposite side and through a binding loop so that the warp threads cross the bottom of the box, like spokes in a wheel, and continue to move around the box until each binding string is holding a warp thread. (See Illustration 23.)

It will be necessary to tie knots in the warp. These ends should be left rather long, so that there will be some flexibility and stretch as the weft is packed down.

Choose several heavy yarns of pleasing colors and alternate them in the weaving. Overlap the ends of the weft threads, and continue the weaving down the sides of the box until all the warp is covered. A coarse-tooth comb is a useful tool to pack the weft in place.

The inside of the box may be lined with velvet glued into place. The handle may be woven of the same yarns as are used for the bag. In this particular instance, the box is not removed. However, one interesting bag was woven on a box by using the entire box and then removing it, adding a tassel at the bottom.

An unusual hat was woven on an ice cream carton, which was removed. Little trinket boxes, woven with bright bits of shiny yarns and metallic threads are original.

23 / Beginning the weft on an oatmeal box

24 / Decorative wrapping on a thorny twig

15

Weaving on Natural Forms

Spider-web-like weaving wrapped around twigs, large pieces of bark, weed stems, flat rocks, and various other forms found in nature holds a fascination for many weavers.

Sometimes finding a natural formation of a branched limb from a tree will suggest a weblike tissue stretched across the limbs. These weaving projects may be found in many exhibitions of creative weaving and may be done on many forms from nature.

A large shell might be drilled with holes, strung with warp and woven to produce a see-through effect with a pink pearl background.

Pieces of bark, twigs, seedpods, stems, and vines have been used in many effective pieces of weaving. Red twig dogwood stems stay remarkably pink even when fully dried. The leaves of the cattail form a tough green weft.

Large room dividers of handspun wool, laced from a

limb hung high to a limb on the floor, form an effective natural screen.

A tripod-shaped twig formation with three limbs pointing down may be used for a table centerpiece or stabile when it is woven or wrapped like a God's-eye.

Although these constructions are not technically weaving in the strictest sense of the word, they are another use of threads to express the weaver's imagination.

16

Using Various Weaving Techniques on Cardboard

When the method of weaving on cardboard has been understood and mastered, the weaver will be aware of the many possibilities of the cardboard loom. In other words, the string lacing to hold the warp and weft in place acts like a loom for needle weaving. Once the warp is in place, many types of weft-weaving are possible. Simple stripes of weft in various colors will produce stripes. Colors taken part way across the warp and interlocked with another color coming in from the other selvage makes an interlocking tapestry. Curved areas can be woven by weaving part way across the warp and turning, making the turn shorter and shorter, with each weft until a curve results. Open areas of warp may be left as vertical lines in a wall hanging.

Knots of various types may be incorporated to add a surface interest. Wrapping several warp threads together with a tightly bound weft thread is an interesting technique.

Back-stitching the weft creates a novel effect as more of the weft is exposed. Twining with two wefts or twining with four wefts forms an interesting texture in contrast to the plain weave. Supplemental warps may be draped across the cardboard loom to be used as the weaver desires.

Trimmings may be added, such as small medallions or God's-eyes, or beads strung on the warp and used at will in the weaving. The picking up of various warp threads in an orderly arrangement will result in the effect of a herringbone weave or twill. These weaves, done in two colors, make an interesting fabric.

Another possibility is the use of fabric dyes to paint or stencil either the warp alone, or the finished fabric. Since the cardboard loom does not require much space, and is also flat, the painting of the warp is quite easy if a blotter is slipped under the warp threads.

If the weft is a finer gauge thread than the warp thread, it can be packed down with a comb and the fabric will be weft-faced. If the weft is a coarser gauge thread than the warp, the fabric has a tendency to become warp-faced. When two warp threads cross two weft threads together, the fabric resembles a basket weave.

When several colors are used for the warp and one single color is used as weft, the stripes become warp

25 / Wrapping the weft around several warps to make openings

stripes, running the length of the fabric. More interesting effects are obtained if the stripes are of varying widths, avoiding monotony by changing the number of threads.

When the colors are used as wefts, the resulting fabric has cross stripes, and here again, variety in size helps to produce a more interesting fabric.

Many interesting effects are gained by tearing fine strips of cotton cloth to be used instead of yarn or thread.

26 / Picking up warps in a staggered pattern to create a herringbone effect

27 / Textures from a variety of weft threads

Appendix

Color Harmony Suggestions

The weaver should be especially alert for yarns and threads which give a fabric a pleasant or, sometimes, unusual texture. There are glossy threads, shiny twists of all colors and gauges, yarns with dull flakes or bumps twisted into the length, loops or metallics added. There is such a variety of yarns, strings, cords, and threads available today that the weaver should be aware of them, just as a painter is constantly searching for particular colors to express himself on canvas.

Sometimes a weaver strikes an unusual effect by using only one color, but combining such a variety of yarn qualities in variations of size, dull or shiny, looped or smooth, that he really seems to be using other colors.

The following color harmony suggestions will present endless variety when one considers the many types of yarn now offered for sale. The more sophisticated weaver will probably want to spin or dye fibers by hand to create unique effects.

Since colors of full intensity are not usually considered harmonious, some attempt at color description is made here.

TRIADS

1. Bright yellow combined with pale blue and pale pink.
2. Bright blue, pale pink, yellow.
3. Bright green, pale orange, pale violet.
4. Bright violet, pale orange, pale green.
5. Yellow-orange, blue-green, red-violet.
6. Blue-violet, yellow-green, red-orange.

ANALOGOUS

1. Dark yellow, yellow-green, brown.
2. Orange, yellow, pale green
3. Red-orange, yellow-green, blue-green.
4. Violet, red-violet, pale red-orange.
5. Violet, pale blue, yellow-green.

MONOCHROMATIC

1. Yellow, ivory, tan, brown.
2. Pale blue, royal-blue, delft-blue, navy.
3. Light pink, rose, wine.
4. Pale green, normal green, dark moss-green.

SINGLE COLOR HARMONIES

1. Red, white, black, gray.
2. Pale gray, light gray, dark gray, bright yellow.
3. Bright red, gray, black.
4. Fuchsia-pink, gray, black.
5. Bright orange, beige, tan, brown.

Glossary

SHED	Opening formed in the warp through which the shuttle is passed.
SHUTTLE	An instrument used for passing the weft thread from one edge of the cloth to the other between the threads of the warp.
WARP	System of threads running lengthwise in loom across which weft threads are passed to form web or cloth.
WEFT	System of threads woven across the warp threads to form cloth.

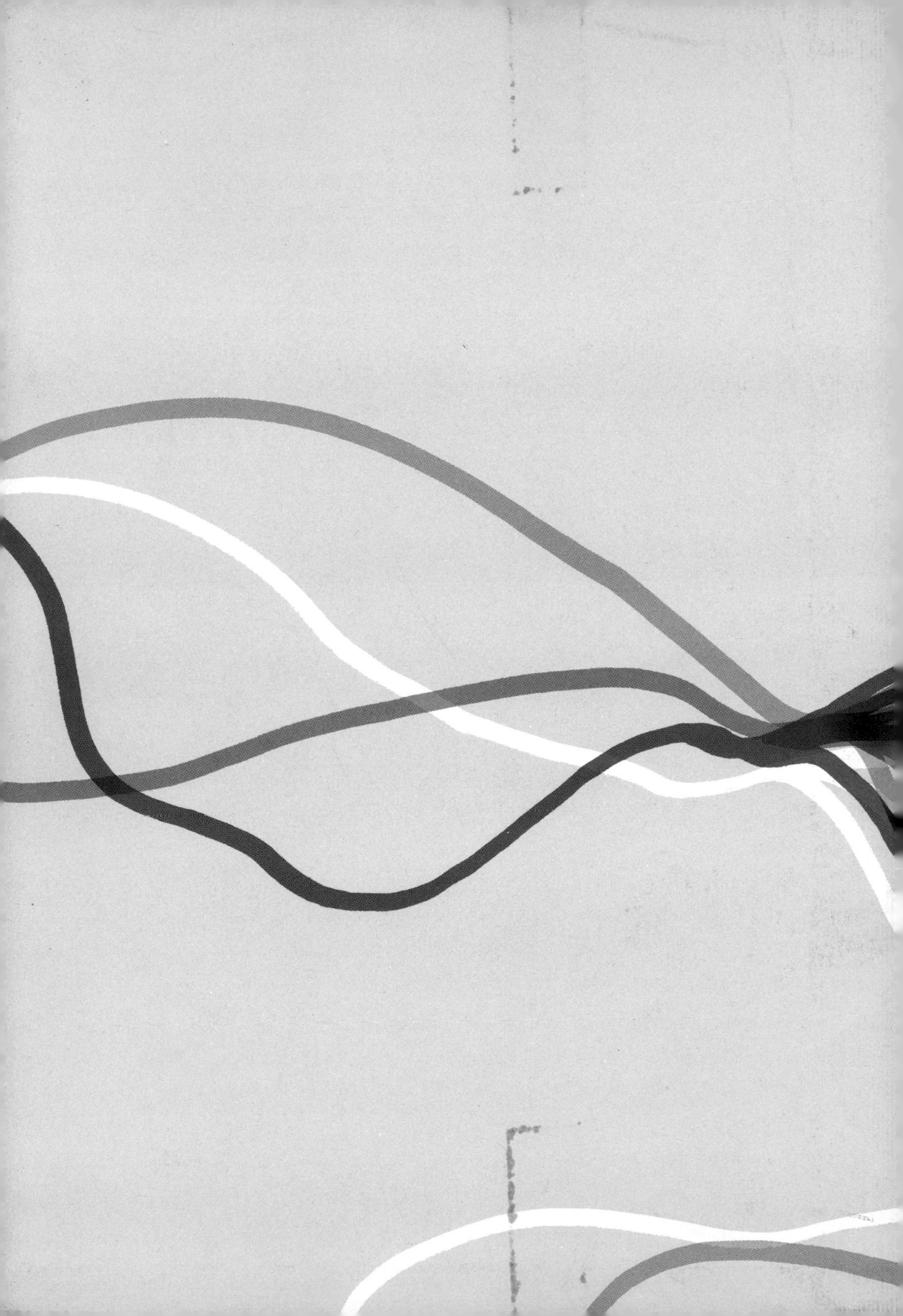